Paper Money

BY DANA MEACHEN RAU

READING CONSULTANT: SUSAN NATIONS, M.ED., AUTHOR/LITERACY COACH/CONSULTANT

WR WEEKLY READER
EARLY LEARNING LIBRARY

Please visit our web site at: **www.earlyliteracy.cc**
For a free color catalog describing Weekly Reader® Early Learning Library's list of high-quality books, call 1-877-445-5824 (USA) or 1-800-387-3178 (Canada). Weekly Reader® Early Learning Library's fax: (414) 336-0164.

Library of Congress Cataloging-in-Publication Data

Rau, Dana Meachen, 1971–
    Paper money / by Dana Meachen Rau.
      p. cm. — (Money and banks)
    Includes bibliographical references and index.
    ISBN 0-8368-4870-5 (lib. bdg.)
    ISBN 0-8368-4877-2 (softcover)
    1. Paper money—United States—Juvenile literature. 2. Dollar, American—Juvenile literature. I. Title. II. Series.
HG591.R32   2005
332.4'044'0973—dc22
                                                2005042204

This edition first published in 2006 by
Weekly Reader® Early Learning Library
A Member of the WRC Media Family of Companies
330 West Olive Street, Suite 100
Milwaukee, WI 53212 USA

Copyright © 2006 by Weekly Reader® Early Learning Library

Editor: Barbara Kiely Miller
Art direction: Tammy West
Cover design and page layout: Dave Kowalski
Picture research: Diane Laska-Swanke

Picture credits: Cover, title, p. 4 Gregg Andersen; pp. 5, 6, 7, 9, 15, 18, 19, 20 (upper left, lower left and right), 21 Diane Laska-Swanke; p. 8 © National Archives/Getty Images; p. 10 © Joe Raedle/Getty Images; pp. 11, 12 (both), 13 (both), 14 (both) © Stock Montage, Inc.; p. 20 (upper right) Courtesy of Dan Laska

Printed in the United States of America

1 2 3 4 5 6 7 8 9 09 08 07 06 05

Table of Contents

You can use a dollar bill to buy many things. With a dollar, you can buy a snack or a drink. You can buy a sheet of stickers or a card for a friend. **Currency** is the money people use to buy things. Coins and paper money are the two forms of currency.

With a dollar bill, you can buy a small toy at the store.

4

Paper money is not really made of paper. It is made of cotton and linen. **Cotton** and **linen** are two kinds of cloth. They are also used to make some kinds of clothes.

When you look closely at a dollar bill, you can see small red and blue threads.

Paper money is used by hundreds of people. Each bill is made to be very strong. A bill is so strong that it will not fall apart if it goes through the wash by mistake. Bills usually last about a year and a half.

After they have been used by many people, bills get worn out.

Paper money is made in seven different amounts.
Some bills are for small amounts of money. They are
one-dollar bills, two-dollar bills, and five-dollar bills.
Other bills are for large amounts. They are ten-dollar
bills, twenty-dollar bills, fifty-dollar bills, and one-
hundred-dollar bills.

The government
makes seven kinds
of bills.

The Bureau of Engraving and Printing, or BEP, makes paper money. It prints money in Washington, D.C., and Fort Worth, Texas. The BEP makes enough bills in one year to circle Earth more than thirty times!

The Bureau of Printing and Engraving Building in Washington, D.C., was built in 1914.

People use one-dollar bills the most. The BEP makes more one-dollar bills than other bills. The one-dollar bill is black and green. Both the twenty-dollar bill and the fifty-dollar bill are more colorful. They are peach and blue as well as black and green.

The twenty-dollar bill is more colorful than the one-dollar bill.

How are bills made? People feed large sheets of paper into a machine called a **printing press**. The printing press works fast. It prints thirty-two bills on each sheet of paper. Another machine cuts the paper into separate bills.

A printing press prints thirty-two bills at a time.

Look at a bill of paper money. Someone is looking back at you! The front of every bill has a picture, or **portrait**, of a famous American. The backs of bills show famous buildings or symbols of America. George Washington's portrait is shown on the one-dollar bill. He was the first president of the United States.

George Washington was president for eight years.

11

The two-dollar bill has a portrait of President Thomas Jefferson. He wrote the Declaration of Independence. The **Declaration of Independence** is an important document in American history. The five-dollar bill shows President Abraham Lincoln. He kept our country together during the Civil War.

Abraham Lincoln (*left*) was the sixteenth president. Thomas Jefferson (*right*) was the third president of the United States.

Andrew Jackson was a very popular president. His portrait is on the twenty-dollar bill. Ulysses S. Grant is on the fifty-dollar bill. He was a famous general who later became president of the United States.

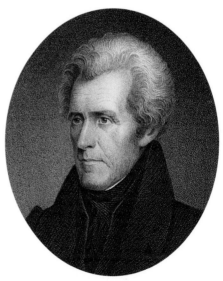

Ulysses S. Grant (*left*) and Andrew Jackson (*right*) were U.S. presidents, too.

Not all bills show presidents. A picture of Alexander Hamilton is on the ten-dollar bill. He was the first Secretary of the Treasury. The **Treasury** is the part of the government in charge of money. Benjamin Franklin is on the one-hundred-dollar bill. He was known for his inventions. He also helped create America's government.

Benjamin Franklin (*left*) and Alexander Hamilton (*right*) were famous Americans.

Look closely at the front of a one-dollar bill. You can learn when the bill was made. Each bill has a serial number, too. This number is a mix of both letters and numbers. The **serial number** tells which batch of money the bill came from. A different serial number is put on every sheet printed, or every thirty-two bills.

Serial number

When bill was made

The front of a dollar bill shows how much the bill is worth. Can you find the words and numbers that give the amount?

On the back of a one-dollar bill, you can see both sides of the Great Seal of America. The left side of the bill shows the back of the Great Seal. It has a pyramid. The pyramid is a symbol for strength. The eye above the pyramid is a symbol for God.

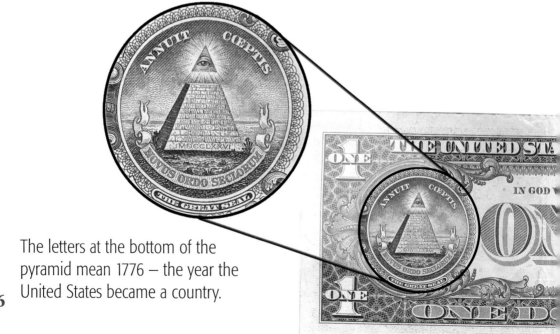

The letters at the bottom of the pyramid mean 1776 – the year the United States became a country.

The right side of the bill shows the front of the Great Seal. It has an eagle. The eagle is holding an olive branch in one **talon**, or claw. It holds arrows in the other. The eagle stands for the United States. The olive branch stands for peace. The arrows stand for war.

The eagle holds thirteen arrows and thirteen olive leaves. They stand for the country's first thirteen states.

Bills also have secrets. When you hold some bills up to a light, you can see another face in the background. This hidden face is called a **watermark**. In the lower right corner, a number is printed in special ink. Its color changes from green to copper when you hold the bill in different directions!

Hidden watermark

A twenty-dollar bill has a hidden portrait on the right side of the bill.

Color changing ink

You can learn a lot from a dollar bill. Paper money has faces and symbols from America's past. These small pieces of paper can help teach you about America's history!

A one-dollar bill has a lot of history on it.

Look at the cost of the items below. Then look at the groups of bills on page 21. Two groups of bills equal the cost of each item. Which ones are they?

1.

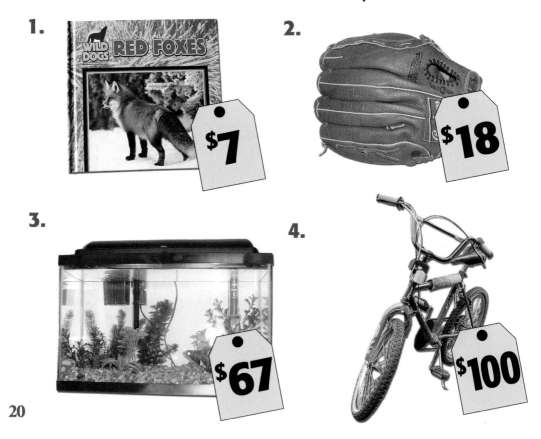

RED FOXES
WILD DOGS

$7

2.

$18

3.

$67

4.

$100

A.

B.

C.

D.

E.

F.

G.

H.

Find the answers on page 23.

21

Glossary

currency – the type of money that is used in a country

general – a leader in the army or other military group

portrait – a picture of someone's head and face

printing press – a machine that prints designs, letters, and numbers on paper

seal – a design used as the official mark of authority by a government, a business, or a person

secretary – the leader of a government department

serial number – a number that tells what place or position something has in a series.

symbols – things that stand for or represent other things

talon – the claw of a bird, such as an eagle

watermark – an image on paper that can be seen only when held up to the light

For More Information

Books

American Coins and Bills. Money Power Discovery Library (series). Jason Cooper (Rourke Publishing)

Dollars. Welcome Books: Money Matters (series). Mary Hill (Children's Press)

How Coins and Bills are Made. Money Power Discovery Library (series). Jason Cooper (Rourke Publishing)

Web Sites

The Bureau of Engraving and Printing
www.moneyfactory.com
Interesting facts about money and new money designs

NIEHS Kids' Pages
www.niehs.nih.gov/kids/triviadollar.htm
The design and symbols on the dollar bill

Math Connection Answers: 1) B and H 2) D and G
3) A and F 4) C and E

Index

About the Author

Dana Meachen Rau is an author, editor, and illustrator.
She has written more than one hundred books for children,
including nonfiction, early readers, and historical fiction.
She lives with her family in Burlington, Connecticut.